WOMEN, CONSCIENCE, AND THE CREATIVE PROCESS

ANNE E. PATRICK

2009 Madeleva Lecture
in Spirituality

Paulist Press
New York/Mahwah, NJ

Book and cover design by Lynn Else

Library of Congress Cataloging-in-Publication Data

Patrick, Anne E.
   Women, conscience, and the creative process / Anne E. Patrick.
      p. cm. — (Madeleva lecture in spirituality ; 2009)
   Includes bibliographical references (p.   ).
   ISBN 978-0-8091-4706-9 (alk. paper)
   1. Christian ethics—Catholic authors. 2. Creative ability—Religious aspects—Catholic Church. 3. Conscience—Religious aspects—Catholic Church. 4. Catholic women—Religious life. I. Title. II. Series.

   BJ1249.P326 2009
   241′.042082—dc22

                                                          2010046120

Published by Paulist Press
997 Macarthur Boulevard
Mahwah, New Jersey 07430

www.paulistpress.com

Printed and bound in the
United States of America

Creative Process WOMEN, CONSCIENCE, AND THE CREATIVE PROCESS **WOMEN, CONSCIENCE, AND THE CREATIVE PROCESS** Women, Conscience, and the Creative Process WOMEN, CONSCIENCE, AND THE CREATIVE PROCESS **WOMEN, CONSCIENCE, AND THE CREATIVE PROCESS** Women, Conscience, and the Creative Process WOMEN, CONSCIENCE, AND THE CREATIVE PROCESS **WOMEN, CONSCIENCE, AND THE CREATIVE PROCESS** Women, Conscience, and the Creative Process WOMEN, CONSCIENCE, AND THE CREATIVE PROCESS **WOMEN, CONSCIENCE, AND THE CREATIVE PROCESS** Women, Conscience, and the Creative Process WOMEN, CONSCIENCE, AND THE CREATIVE PROCESS **WOMEN, CONSCIENCE, AND THE CREATIVE PROCESS** Women, Conscience, and the Creative Process WOMEN, CONSCIENCE, AND THE CREATIVE PROCESS **WOMEN, CONSCIENCE, AND THE CREATIVE PROCESS** Women, Conscience, and the Creative Process WOMEN, CONSCIENCE, AND THE CREATIVE PROCESS **WOMEN, CONSCIENCE, AND THE CREATIVE PROCESS** Women, Conscience, and the Creative Process WOMEN, CONSCIENCE, AND THE CREATIVE PROCESS **WOMEN, CONSCIENCE, AND THE CREATIVE PROCESS** Women, Conscience, and the Creative Process WOMEN, CONSCIENCE, AND THE

To my students and colleagues
at Carleton College,
who for thirty years have provided me with
a creative community of intellectual
and artistic exploration.
And to the Sisters of the Holy Names
of Jesus and Mary,
who for fifty years have provided me with
a community of shared mission,
friendship, and inspiration.

Anne E. Patrick, SNJM, is William H. Laird Professor of Religion and the Liberal Arts, *emerita*, at Carleton College (Northfield, Minnesota), where from 1980 to 2009 she taught courses in Christian ethics, Catholicism, feminist and liberation theologies, and religion and literature. She has held visiting professorships at St. John's University (New York) and the University of Tulsa, and has also taught at the University of Chicago Divinity School and several academies in the eastern United States. Originally from Washington, DC, she studied at Medaille College (BA), the University of Maryland (MA, English), and the University of Chicago (MA, Divinity, and PhD, Religion and Literature). She is a member of the Sisters of the Holy Names of Jesus and Mary, a past president of the Catholic Theological Society of America, and a founding vice president of the International Network of Societies for Catholic Theology. She has been a director of the Society of Christian Ethics, an editor for the Religious Book Club, and a columnist for *Liturgy*. As chair of the Committee on Women in Church and Society of the National Assembly of Women Religious, she helped to plan the 1975 Women's Ordination Conference. Her writings on religious, ethical, and literary topics have appeared in many books and periodicals, and she is the author of *Liberating Conscience: Feminist Explorations in Catholic Moral Theology* (Continuum, 1996). She is now completing *Conscience in Context: Vocation, Virtue, and History* (Continuum International, forthcoming).

CONTENTS

ACKNOWLEDGMENTS

Special thanks to Carleton College, and its then-President Rob Oden, Dean H. Scott Bierman, and Religion Department Chair Roger Jackson, for a leave from teaching in 2008–9 that enabled me to continue my research and writing while receiving treatment for cancer. I am grateful also to Kathleen Dolphin, PBVM, director of the Center for Spirituality at Saint Mary's College, for the invitation to give the 2009 Madeleva Lecture, and to her and Nancy de Flon of Paulist Press for their encouragement as I pursued this topic. I thank as well the Studium, Spirituality Center, and sisters of St. Benedict's Monastery in St. Joseph, Minnesota, for the many ways they have fostered my creative efforts over the years. Finally, I thank several friends whose close readings of the manuscript at various stages were especially helpful: Mara Faulkner, OSB; Joan Cook, SC; Anita M. Pampusch; and Carol A. Tauer.

INTRODUCTION

In her 2009 memoir, *The Blue Sweater: Bridging the Gap between Rich and Poor in an Interconnected World*, Jacqueline Novogratz tells of the influence of her first-grade teacher, Sister Mary Theophane:

> Sister was known as one of the kindest of the nuns, though she had high expectations for content —and handwriting. If we earned a perfect test score, she'd hand us a card with a summary of the life of a saint printed on it, and I studied diligently to collect as many cards as I could. I found their lives an inspiration....

Sister also inspired the impressionable six-year-old by hanging a poster on the classroom wall of hands holding a rice bowl, which led to her interest in the lives of Chinese children and in traveling abroad. Not surprisingly, at one point she voiced the desire to become a nun like her teacher. On hearing this, Sister Mary Theophane "enfolded me in her thick black robes and told me I was just a child, but it was a lovely idea. 'Regardless of what you become,' she said, 'remember always that to whom much is given, much is expected. God gave you many gifts and it is important that you use them for others as best you can.'"[1]

This teacher was reinforcing values that Novogratz had learned at home, particularly about diligence and concern for others. As she notes in the book's dedication, "My family helped make me who I am...and they join me in dedicating this book to our larger family, those countless millions around the world who lack money and security but possess dignity and an indomitable spirit."[2] If Sister Mary Theophane is alive today and able to read her pupil's memoir, she would surely delight in what has become of Jacqueline, who absorbed her early lessons about kindness involving high expectations, accountability, and reward for measurable success, and incorporated them into her postcollege search for truly effective ways of assisting the world's poor to improve their lives. Challenges and setbacks would teach her much more along the way, but before she turned forty, Novogratz had established a world-changing philanthropic organization, the Acumen Fund, which by 2008 was managing more than $40 million of investments in forty enterprises benefiting the poor, including projects designed to bring safe water, housing, alternative energy, information and communications technology, and health care to persons in the developing world.[3]

Novogratz also has an eye for style and beauty, and often her memoir describes the clothes that she and others are wearing. The book's title, in fact, celebrates the way a sweater she had received from her uncle came to reinforce the lesson learned in childhood about interconnectedness. She had worn this favorite sweater, woven of blue wool with images of zebras against a snow-capped mountain, for several years until she outgrew it. Then, when she was in high school, she gave it to Goodwill and largely forgot about it. After graduating from college and starting a career in international banking, however, she was in Rwanda to assist with a microfinance project for women, when she happened to see a skinny young boy wearing *her* blue sweater. Amazed, she stopped the boy, looked inside his collar, and found her name still there on the tag. The incident was life-shaping for Novogratz:

> The story of the blue sweater has always reminded me of how we are all connected. Our actions—and inaction—touch people every day across the globe, people we may never know and never meet....Seeing my sweater on that child renewed my sense of purpose in Africa. At that point in my own journey, my worldview was shifting. I'd begun my career as an international banker, discovering the power of capital, of mar-

3

kets, *and* of politics, as well as how the poor are so often excluded from all three. I wanted to understand better what stands between poverty and wealth.[4]

In the years that followed, Novogratz continued to learn from her work with various African projects. She also earned a master's degree in business at Stanford University and gained experience directing philanthropy and leadership programs at the Rockefeller Foundation. Then, in 2001, after acquiring $10 million from corporate and individual "investors," she launched her own organization, the Acumen Fund. Her idea was to transform traditional donor-grantee relationships by emphasizing that charitable gifts were investments that would earn a return in social change. Convinced that much charitable aid contributed to corruption and did little actually to improve the circumstances of the poor, Novogratz insisted on funding projects that regarded the poor as "customers," as agents who were willing to pay prices within their means for things they needed. "My passion," she wrote, "was using business models to create effective, sustainable systems where government or charity alone had failed poor people." She elaborated on the fund thus:

I began to think of what we were launching as a venture capital fund for the poor. We would raise charitable funds, then invest equity, loans, and grants—whatever was needed—in organizations led by visionary entrepreneurs who were delivering to low-income communities services such as safe water, health care, housing, and alternative energy sources. In addition, we would provide them with wide-ranging support on everything from basic business planning, to hiring managers, to helping them connect to markets. We would measure the results of our investment not only in the capital flowing back to the fund, but also— and more importantly—in the investment's social impact. Any money returned would then be reinvested into other enterprises that served the poor.[5]

The Acumen Fund involves what Novogratz calls "patient capitalism," which is not in a rush for financial returns but seeks large-scale improvement in the lives of poor people. Its approach is to combine the generosity of charity with the realism of proven business models that demand transparency, accountability, and concrete measures of success. The fund supports creative entrepreneurs with "passion, commitment, and big ideas," in the hope that the best ideas can be "taken to scale" and implemented through institutions that will outlive their founders and continue to be widely effective for social progress. For example, Novogratz was impressed by Satyan Mishra, "a visionary entrepreneur who was focused first and foremost on supporting the poor by building a large-scale information distribution system" in his native India through the establishment of a network of stores ("tele-kiosks") where a local owner would set up shop with a computer, telephone, and camera, and sell various services to the villagers.[6] His for-profit company, Drishtee, had five hundred kiosks when Acumen invested in it and also provided a loan for expansion. By 2007 there were two thousand kiosks, and by the fall of 2008, according to Novogratz:

> the company was operating in more than 4,000 villages, creating more than 5,300 jobs and serving 7.5 million. What thrills me just as much is that the company is building a powerful distribution system through which it ultimately will be able to sell a multitude of products that can improve a low-income person's ability to change his or her own life.[7]

Earlier in India, Acumen had provided capital for the noted surgeon Dr. Govindappa Venkataswamy to expand operations at his Aravind Eye Hospital through the use of "telemedicine." Already doctors at this hospital were restoring vision to thousands of cataract patients yearly on a generous sliding payment scale, and Venkataswamy wanted to use computers with video capability both for diagnosis of patients who live far from medical centers, and also for training doctors in the best surgical techniques. By 2008, Novogratz observes, telemedicine "had been integrated into 16 vision centers in rural villages, each providing about 50,000 people with access in places where individuals previously had no access to high-quality eye care—and Aravind was treating about 150,000 patients a year."[8]

The "patient capital" of Acumen Fund has also supported entrepreneurs who have developed systems for purifying and marketing drinking water the poor can afford, and designed effective ways of preventing malaria, among other enterprises. Its overall aim is to invest in creative individuals who combine great humanitarian ambitions with business know-how, willingness to risk, and ability to learn from customers and results.

Something that intrigues me about Novogratz's book is the way the Catholicism that so clearly influenced her in childhood is not mentioned as a source of inspiration in the latter part of her memoir. As she brings the book to a conclusion, however, she recalls a conversation with Dr. Venkataswamy shortly before his death at age eighty-seven in which she asked him about his views on God. He answered after a moment of silence:

> For me, God exists in that place where all living things are interconnected—and we know it when we feel the divine. For the world to heal its suffering, we need to combine tough determination

and bring solutions to poverty with this sense of ourselves not as isolated individuals, but as beings who need one another and depend on one another.[9]

In this stress on interconnectedness and the need to use gifts effectively for others, I see the continuing influence of Sister Mary Theophane's words and her classroom poster of the rice bowl. As an adult, Novogratz no longer relies on cards about official saints for inspiration, but she does take inspiration from many sources nonetheless, and particularly from persons like Venkataswamy and her mentor at Stanford, the founder of Common Cause, John Gardner. In her experience, such persons have not only enjoyed a sense of "purpose, meaning, and happiness" in their own lives, but have also "created legacies that will long outlast them, for their visions for change were based not on their own egos but on contributing to the world in a way that released the energies of millions of people."[10]

Under such influences, Novogratz has come to express her twofold sense of what is required for a positive future for everyone on Earth. "The first step for each of us," she writes, "is to develop our own moral imagination, the ability to put ourselves in another person's shoes....Our work should remind us all that the poor the world over are our brothers and sisters." Empathy alone, however, is not enough. The world also needs persons with "tangible skills," "focus and conviction," "hard-headed analysis," and courage.[11] Novogratz uses no specifically religious language here, but I find her ideals quite congruent with the results-oriented language with which the Jesus of Matthew's Gospel declares who will be rewarded at the Last Judgment. When all is said and done, the kingdom will be inherited by those with the imagination to see, and the generosity and ability to respond effectively to, their neighbors in need: "For I was hungry and you gave me food, I was thirsty and you gave me something to drink, I was a stranger and you welcomed me, I was naked and you gave me clothing, I was sick and you took care of me, I was in prison and you visited me" (25:35–36).

When I think about Novogratz's ideals and accomplishments I find them a striking example of the approach to the moral life that the Second Vatican Council document *Optatam Totius* sought to encourage, namely, one stressing the obligation of the faithful to "bring forth fruit in charity for the life of the world."[12] Her memoir also exemplifies the "option for the poor" that church leaders have stressed in Catholic social teaching since the council. Although *The Blue Sweater* does not pretend to be a work in Christian ethics, nor does it build on the Christian scriptures, it does illustrate how one woman's creativity has been directed to achieving significant good in the world. In this

9

respect it reminds us of Sister Mary Madeleva Wolff, CSC, the innovative educator of women for whom this lecture series is named. As a college president, as a poet and professor of literature, as an influential moral agent, and indeed as a creatively responsible woman of God, Sister Madeleva has inspired the creativity of many for nearly a century, not least among them the Saint Mary's College community and the Madeleva Lecturers and their readers.

In the present work, *Women, Conscience, and the Creative Process*, readers of previous lectures will detect the influence of certain of these small books, beginning with the 1985 lecture that opened the series, in which Monika Hellwig commended to Christian women who would help a troubled world a spirituality of "prayer, compassion, solidarity, and creative imagination."[13] Hellwig declared that Christian women of this era "have a calling to preserve their freedom of spirit in using the creative imagination, in the way that they have possessed it in their socially and politically powerless past, but at the same time to express that freedom and creativity with power in the public sphere" for the sake of world peace and social justice.[14] Six years later Dolores Leckey invited sustained reflection on *Women and Creativity* by exploring three places that have in the past fostered women's creativity—namely, the convent, the home, and the Women's Movement.

She went on to say that today an alliance of lay and religious women could do much to improve the home of the global human family by caring for the Earth, developing true partnership between the sexes, and finding ways to advocate for children beyond our immediate circles, especially those suffering from poverty, illness, and violence.[15] More recently, M. Shawn Copeland's 2007 lecture identified creativity as one of the qualities that enabled the founder of the Sisters of the Holy Family, Henriette Delille, to transcend the limits that racism and sexism had imposed on her life, and in 2008, Barbara Fiand's work on the interface between science and spirituality showed that in a continuously evolving universe our relationship with the Divine Creator requires active participation in creation. As Fiand observed, God's creative energy is "focused in us by virtue of the freedom and consciousness that makes us who we are."[16]

These and a number of other Madeleva Lecturers have made tantalizing references to creativity.[17] Here I draw out more explicitly the significance of this topic of creativity and the creative process for the Christian moral life, and especially the moral lives of Catholic women, who today experience some tension among ourselves and in some cases with church leaders over matters of what we call "conscience." I suggest that the quality of creativity, at least in the form of creative responsibility, should be numbered among the virtues we ought to cultivate as

Christians, along with honesty, justice, courage, and other strengths of character. In making this case I discuss four topics: (1) Discipleship and the Call to Creativity; (2) Creativity and the Creative Process; (3) *Conscience* as a Contested Term; and (4) Conscience as the Creatively Responsible Self. I am linking these topics of discipleship, conscience, responsibility, and the creative process because I have long believed that powers of imagination and willingness to risk new approaches to problems are essential for the Christian moral life, and that a creative approach to responsibility is needed if we are to fulfill our vocation to "bring forth fruit in charity for the life of the world" (*Optatam Totius*, no. 16).

I

DISCIPLESHIP AND THE CALL TO CREATIVITY

The *Catechism of the Catholic Church* describes the life of the Christian in scriptural terms that have long inspired the baptized: "Following Christ and united with him, Christians can strive to be 'imitators of God as beloved children, and walk in love' [Eph 5:1–2] by conforming their thoughts, words and actions to the 'mind...which is yours in Christ Jesus,' [Phil 2:5] and by following his example." Indeed, according to John's Gospel, after washing the feet of his disciples at the Last Supper, Jesus declares, "For I have set you an example, that you also should do as I have done to you" (13:15).[18]

While affirming this tradition of the *imitatio Christi*, I want to ask whether the interpretation of such texts has overly stressed the passive aspects of imitating Christ Jesus and being conformed to his mind, while neglecting to foster the creativity that Jesus himself exemplified in the gospel narratives. Moreover, the ideal of following and imitating Jesus has often been interpreted in a literalistic way that does not take account of the complex background out of which the gospel stories developed. In fact, it is not so easy to see the Jesus of the Gospels for who he really is, and this complicates our attempts to do what Paul instructs the Philippians, to "live your life in a manner worthy of the gospel of Christ" (1:27). As William Spohn observes in *Go and Do Likewise: Jesus and Ethics*, "Christians have often substituted a false norm for the story of Jesus by projecting their own values and biases onto it." He elaborates:

> The sentimental Jesus of middle-class piety hides the cross of poverty and oppression; the Jesus of Western imperialism is refuted by the nonviolence of the passion accounts; the Jesus of patriarchal tradition wilts under the evidence that the Nazarene chose the powerless and marginalized to share his table.[19]

To understand the Jesus of the Gospels in relation to the question of the need for creativity in the moral life, we need to understand the social, religious, and political situation in which he lived, for his words are in the first place addressed to the hopes and fears of his contemporaries. This deepening of understanding is the task of a lifetime, and the availability of good studies today makes it possible to gain insight on a regular basis. One resource I would mention beyond the excellent work by Spohn is Walter Wink's small volume, *Jesus and Nonviolence: The Third Way*, which emphasizes the creativity of Jesus in response to the challenging circumstances he faced during his ministry. A reinterpretation of Matthew 5:38–41 is crucial to his argument that Jesus rejected both violence and passive submission to evil in favor of a "third way," a creative way of resisting evil and seeking change. This passage has both inspired and troubled Christians:

> You have heard that it was said, "An eye for an eye and a tooth for a tooth." But I say to you: Do not resist an evildoer. But if anyone strikes you on the right cheek, turn the other also; and if anyone wants to sue you and take your coat, give your cloak as well; and if anyone forces you to go one mile, go also the second mile.[20]

Feminists especially have taken issue with these sayings, objecting to the submissiveness to evil they seem to advocate. Can Jesus really be asking abused spouses to "turn the other cheek," we inquire, and we rather quickly assume this saying has little relevance for those who suffer oppression at the hands of the powerful. Wink, however, puts these hard sayings into their cultural context, and lets them take on a very different meaning. He shows that these three responses to an evildoer are actually creative ways of resisting, which in time may lead to change.

Wink first reminds the reader how violent and oppressive things were for Jews during the years of Jesus' life. Jesus and his friends would have been well aware that an armed revolt against the Romans in Galilee had led to a crushing defeat for the Jews, some two thousand of whom were crucified along the roads of the region. Likewise, during Jesus' youth, a Jewish assault on a Roman arsenal at Sepphoris, just three miles from Nazareth, had failed, and citizens who supported the revolt had been sold into slavery. Wink believes that Jesus saw the futility of trying to use force in these circumstances, but this did not mean he advocated passivity and nonresistance to evil. In fact, Wink points out that the Greek word rendered by King James and most subsequent translators as "*Do not resist* [an evildoer]"—*antistēnai*—usually has a *military* meaning in the Greek Old Testament, and that Jesus' words would be better translated as, "Don't strike back at evil (or the one who has done you evil) in kind."[21] Far from advocating "impractical idealism" or "doormat" passivity, Jesus wanted his followers to use strategies that would resist evil more creatively and effectively than by brute force.[22] To make this clear, Jesus follows his injunction not to respond to evil in kind by offering three examples of the sort of resistance he does recommend. Wink regards these as a "jujitsu" way of opposing evil, a creative response that changes the dynamics of an oppressive relationship and turns the power of an evildoer against himself.

Most who hear these examples today, however, fail to understand their meaning, because we do not know enough about the cultural context in which Jesus provided them. Jesus' first example of a nonviolent response to evil involves someone who is struck on the *right* cheek. As Wink observes, in this culture the left hand was used only for unclean tasks, and a person of dignity would strike another only with the right hand. Therefore, the blow in question could not come from a fist fight, for a blow from the right fist would land on the *left* cheek of an opponent. Instead, to hit the right cheek of someone with the right hand requires a backhand slap, and this was clearly an insult, something done to humiliate another rather than to cause injury. Such a backhand slap should not happen between equals; Wink notes that the later Rabbinic legal code, the Mishnah, continued the tradition of making a great distinction between the fines for different types of striking a peer. To hit a peer with one's fist resulted in a fine of 4 zuz, but to slap a peer with the back of one's hand led to a fine of 400 zuz. What Jesus was talking about here, then, was a culturally specific gesture, a slap with the back of one's good hand, which was the usual way of putting inferiors in their place. As Wink declares, "Masters back-handed slaves; husbands, wives; parents, children; men, women; Romans, Jews. *We have here a set of unequal relations, in each of which retaliation would be suicidal.* The only normal response would be cowering submission."[23] And cowering submission is precisely what Jesus does *not* recommend. Instead, Jesus advocates presenting the *other* cheek, which in this culture is a creative way of changing the power dynamics. Wink explains: "The person who turns the other cheek is saying, in effect, 'Try again. Your first blow failed to achieve its intended effect. I deny you the power to humiliate me. I am a human being just like you. Your status does not alter that fact. You cannot demean me.'" He goes on to point out that the action creates "enormous difficulties" for the oppressor:

> He cannot use the backhand because his nose is in the way. He can't use his left hand regardless. If he hits with a fist, he makes himself an equal, acknowledging the other as a peer....The oppressor has been forced, against his will, to regard this subordinate as an equal human being. The powerful person has been stripped of his power to dehumanize the other. This response [of turning the other cheek], far from admonishing passivity and cowardice, is an act of defiance.[24]

It likewise helps to understand the cultural context of Jesus' second example, the one about dealing with someone who would take you to court to sue for your outer garment. The Book of Deuteronomy had placed some limits on how Jews should relate to debtors, and chapter 24 stipulates that if a poor man has pledged his outer garment to guarantee repayment of a loan, this garment must be returned to him at sundown so that he can use it as a cover for sleeping. Wink has noted that "indebtedness was the most serious social problem in first-century Palestine," a problem that was "the direct consequence of Roman imperial policy," which involved multiple layers of taxation to support wars and enrich the powerful.[25] Jesus is well aware of this problem and makes many references to debtors in his teachings. Why, then, Wink asks, does Jesus advise people to give the creditor their inner garment as well as their outer one? Because this leaves them naked, and in the culture of Jesus' time this was more embarrassing for the beholder than for the naked person. Recall that the curse of Ham (and Canaan) (Gen 9:20–27) fell on the one who saw his father's nakedness, not on Noah who was naked.

Wink maintains that the debtor's surrendering of his inner garment is quite the opposite of tolerating injustice. Instead, the debtor has ridiculed the unjust law, shown the creditor to be complicit in injustice, and in the process challenged him to repent. Wink believes that this "hard saying" of Jesus is actually a suggestion to use strategies of clowning and satire to challenge the power of oppressors. Its message is "a practical, strategic measure for empowering the oppressed."[26] And he gives an example from recent history of how such a strategy can sometimes work. He recalls an instance when the South African enforcers of apartheid were ready to bulldoze a shanty town after most of the workers had gone to their jobs. The few women remaining decided to strip off their clothing, and the army backed off.

Finally, knowing the cultural context of Jesus' third example of how to respond to injustice helps us see new meaning in the injunction, "if anyone forces you to go one mile, go also the second mile." Here Jesus was referring to a policy of the occupying army that Galileans would have known well. Roman soldiers were allowed to force civilians to carry their packs for just one mile. There were mile markers along the roads, and soldiers who tried to make civilians assist them beyond one mile were subject to heavy penalties. From the empire's perspective, this limit was a way of allowing the armies to make progress without angering the local populations too much. According to Wink, Jesus knew that outright revolt against the occupying forces would not have been effective, and his words were meant to show "how the oppressed can recover the initiative, how they can assert their human dignity in a situation that cannot for the time being be changed. The rules are Caesar's, but not how one responds to the rules—that is God's, and Caesar has no power over that."[27]

An offer to carry the pack a second mile is disconcerting for the soldier. Are you trying to get him into trouble? As Wink observes,

> From a situation of servile impressments, you have once more seized the initiative. You have taken back the power of choice. The soldier is thrown off-balance by being deprived of the predictability of your response....Imagine the hilarious situation of a Roman infantryman pleading with a Jew, "Aw, come on, please give me back my pack!"[28]

Wink believes that all three examples have been misunderstood because their context is not known, and they are taken too literally. As I have indicated, all three responses—turning the other cheek, giving up the inner garment as well as the outer one, and going the extra mile—are in fact ways of responding to evil that are creative and transformative. At the very least they restore dignity and initiative to the oppressed, and they also have the potential to expose the oppression to public scrutiny and perhaps to shame the oppressor into repentance. And in time, such aikido-like responses may lead to real change.

I think the contemporary Womenpriests Movement shares some affinity with what Wink has been calling the "Third Way" of Jesus, that is, a way of responding to oppression that is beyond both violence and cowering submission. Ever since the Second Vatican Council declared in *Gaudium et Spes* #29 that because of the essential equality of all persons, "every type of discrimination, whether social or cultural, whether based on sex, race, color, social condition, language or religion, is to be overcome and eradicated as contrary to God's intent," there has been growing interest in the possibility of ordaining women, with many Catholics contending that the council's words should apply to church structures as well as to secular societies.[29] While the Vatican continues to oppose even the discussion of such change, some Catholic women have felt called to ordained ministry, and have studied theology and entered ministerial service as chaplains or employees of parishes and dioceses. Their general exclusion from sacramental ministry, however, has been experienced as an injustice by many, who believe God is calling women to sacramental service and leadership, but man-made traditions are preventing them from answering fully. Since 1975 there has been an organized Women's Ordination Movement in the United States, and in 2002 seven women took matters a step further and were ordained in Europe by an Argentine bishop no longer in communion with Rome. Although Pope John Paul II sent notice of excommunication to the "Danube 7," they sent a formal response declaring their refusal to accept this status and claiming full membership in the church. Since then two, perhaps three, Catholic bishops in good standing have secretly ordained several of the womenpriests as bishops, carefully following official procedures and placing the documents in a safe-deposit box, and these womenbishops have gone on to ordain deacons, priests, and bishops themselves.[30]

It remains to be seen what will result from the Womenpriests Movement, but to date it has survived the efforts of the hierarchy to quash it, and for those who believe the current status of women in Catholicism is not a just one, the movement represents a creative and nonviolent attempt to overcome oppression that bears some resemblance to the examples Jesus gave in a very different context. By creating a system of recognizing candidates who meet appropriate criteria for ordination, and by celebrating the ministries of women who are actually serving in diaconal, priestly, and episcopal ways, the movement seizes "the moral initiative" and models a "creative alternative" to the all-male clerical system; women involved in the movement break the cycle of humiliation by refusing to accept an inferior position, and by refusing to regard excommunication as separating them from the church. The public nature of their action helps to "expose the injustice of the system," and perhaps, in time, will "shame the oppressor into repentance."[31] The jury is still out on whether in a century or two the leaders of this movement will be thought of as more like Catherine of Siena or Martin Luther, and my belief is that the words of Gamaliel in the first century concerning the preaching of Peter are relevant to the current situation: "For if this idea of theirs or its execution is of human origin, it will collapse; but if it is from God, you will never be able to put them down..." (Acts 5:38–39).

Whether or not one agrees with this interpretation of the Womenpriests Movement, the important thing is to recognize that the gospel stories themselves invite Christians to cultivate creativity in their own moral lives. Spohn names his study of Jesus and ethics *Go and Do Likewise*, creatively applying the conclusion of Jesus' Parable of the Good Samaritan (Luke 10:25–37). In this familiar passage, Luke describes how Jesus is asked by a lawyer about the meaning of the commandment to "love your neighbor as yourself." Instead of providing a definition, Jesus responds with the story of a man who was beaten and left for dead on the road to Jericho, and then neglected by a priest and a Levite, but attended to with kindness and generosity by a despised Samaritan, who even leaves money for an innkeeper to use for further care. After telling the story, Jesus asks this question: "Which of these three, do you think, was a neighbor to the man who fell into the hands of the robbers?" to which the lawyer replied, "The one who showed him mercy." It is then that Jesus replies, "Go and do likewise" (vv. 36–37).

The central task for Christian ethics, in Spohn's view, is contained in the word *likewise*. Disciples are to be followers of Jesus, not clones who seek to replicate his words and deeds exactly. Spohn placed great emphasis on something called the "analogical imagination," which involves the ability of disciples to relate to Jesus as a model in such a way that our lives are both similar to and different from that of Jesus. Spohn sought to retain the emotional power of the *imitatio Christi* approach to the moral life, while avoiding the literalism and sentimentality associated with bracelets that would reduce discernment to the simplistic question, "What Would Jesus Do?" "The danger of some 'imitation of Christ' spiritualities," he declared in a 1994 lecture on "Jesus and Ethics," "is that they terminate in the person of Jesus, like worshipping an icon, whereas the Jesus of the Gospels was radically concerned [not about himself but] about God" and "the breaking in of the Reign of God and the people most in need of justice and reconciliation."[32] For Spohn, as for H. Richard Niebuhr, a theologian he greatly admired, Jesus was like a "Rosetta Stone" that supplies the key to decoding what God is enabling and requiring each uniquely gifted Christian to be and to do in a different age.

As Spohn put it,

> Jesus did not come teaching timeless truths or a
> uniform way of life to be replicated in every gen-
> eration. Rather his words, encounters, and life
> story set patterns that can be flexibly but faith-
> fully extended to new circumstances. These pat-
> terns lead us to envision analogous ways of acting
> that are partly the same and partly different.[33]

In other words, for Spohn Jesus supplies a para-
digm, not a blueprint, and thus his title is "Go and
do likewise," not "Go and do exactly the same,"
much less "Go and do whatever you want."[34]

To illustrate this idea of creatively imagining
what the example of Jesus might suggest to contemporary believers, Spohn reflects on Christian
efforts to act in ways inspired by what Jesus did in
washing his disciples' feet at the Last Supper.
John's Gospel describes what Jesus did (13:1–3).
As Spohn interprets this text:

> Loving his own to the end, [Jesus] gets up from
> the table, takes off his outer robe, takes up the
> towel and bowl of a servant, and washes the feet
> of his disciples. They are dumbfounded and
> appalled. This act of hospitality belonged to a
> Gentile slave, someone who would not be con-
> taminated by the impurity that clung to bare feet.
> The master is turning their world upside down.[35]

He goes on to observe that Jesus' words, "Just as I have loved you, you also should love one another. By this everyone will know you for my disciples, if you have love for one another" (13:34–35) entail that from this point on the community of his followers should function as the sign of God's love and salvation. However, and this is the point that connects Spohn with the Wink book discussed earlier, the disciples are not to take Jesus too literally here. As Spohn puts it, "If the disciples had taken Jesus literally, Christians would be washing feet every Sunday. They knew better than to copy him. He had given them an example, a demonstration, which graphically pointed to a distinctive way of loving service. They had to figure out from this sign how they could become a corresponding sign to the world." In other words, they had to use their imaginations, and rather than ask, "What would Jesus do?" they should inquire, "what creative response to my circumstances does the word or example of Jesus suggest to me?"[36] To illustrate this idea Spohn describes three Holy Thursday services that each attempt to reflect the essence of what Jesus did with his disciples.

The first is at St. Peter's in Rome, where each Holy Thursday the pope washes the feet of twelve men. The second is at Holy Spirit Parish in Berkeley, where on Holy Thursday the pastor removes his chasuble and puts it on the altar, and then washes the feet of a woman from the parish, who then washes his feet. Then the two of them wash the feet of twelve other men and women in the congregation. The third service takes place in a Baltimore church, where the Irish American pastor removes his chasuble and then shines the shoes of twelve elderly African American men. To Spohn, although the papal ritual is very traditional and follows the Gospel rather closely, it "may be the least faithful to the message," especially because of the exclusion of women. He finds the example from the Berkeley parish more praiseworthy because the footwashing ceremony "highlights not the person of the pastor but the responsibility of all to follow the example of Jesus," and "the prominence of women and children highlights the radical equality of the Christian vocation."[37] But it is the third ritual that Spohn believes may be closest to the spirit of what Jesus demonstrated with his disciples, even though neither washing nor water is involved, because it is a real reversal of roles in our culture when a well-educated white American male does the work of shining the shoes of men of color.

We may see other values in all three of the rituals, and our interpretations may differ from that of Spohn, but what is important here is his conclusion that "Christian moral reflection tries to imagine actions that will be appropriate to the problem at hand and faithful to the story of Jesus."[38] If the actions are fitting, they will be analogous to the actions of Jesus, similar and at the same time different; like the actions of Jesus, but not exactly the same. "The story of Jesus," he emphasizes, "cannot be copied univocally, like a timeless blueprint. There are many ways to be Christian, just as there are four Gospels."[39] This entails that Christians will not always agree on what actions are most appropriate in a given situation, though we are always accountable to the same story and values of the Gospels. There will be much that can be agreed upon, but also some diversity, because Christian ethics involves both being faithful to the story of Jesus and at the same time being creative in applying his values and teachings to the circumstances of our day.

Spohn was convinced that attending to the example of Jesus in a nonliteral way would empower the Christian imagination to see what God is doing in our world and would inspire fitting responses to God's ongoing invitations. He had practical advice for cultivating this sort of imagination. Christians must *experience* what the Gospels are getting at in ways that affect their emotional lives profoundly, for that is the only way to learn how to be a disciple of Jesus. "Like the palate of a good chef," he wrote in a 2005 essay, "the discriminating judgment of the Christian can be trained."[40] Spohn saw spiritual practices as basic to this training for conversion of life, which is a gradual process involving changes in our perception and our dispositions, and thus in our identity. By practices he meant "committed exercises, activities that we deliberately set aside time to do regularly," such as eucharistic worship, forgiveness, lobbying for social justice, working in a soup kitchen, and prayer.[41] What Spohn said about the practice of prayer is, I think, increasingly important in our era of constant electronic connectivity:

*Prayer is the place where we can hear the harmony that discernment seeks....*The practice of Christian discernment helps us develop that well-tuned ear. The tuning fork is the life of Christ as presented in the Gospels and present in faith. Prayer is the place where we can best hear the dominant tone of that tuning fork. No piano tuner has a radio playing while he is trying to work.[42]

To extend the metaphor, the story of Jesus does not tell us directly what to do in our circumstances, but by attending faithfully to that tuning fork we are in a position to hear what God summons us to accomplish in our own time and are given the strength to do it while we have life. We will not always be able to succeed in accomplishing the good we envision or transforming the evils we experience—Jesus did not know such success in his lifetime—but Jesus has shown us how to invent solutions to dilemmas, how to inspire and challenge others, how to confront evil creatively, and how to trust in God's faithfulness despite the evils and tragedies of history.

The ideal of *imitatio Christi*, in sum, involves much more than obedience to commandments and conformity to social expectations. The creative Jesus who invented stories and knew when to observe rules and when to go beyond them for the sake of neighbors in need is best followed by disciples whose spiritual practices include the nurturing of imagination and creativity. Theologian Dorothee Soelle envisioned a transformation of Christian ethics based on such an understanding, and argued in her 1968 work *Beyond Mere Obedience* for the need to regard imagination as basic to virtue, and to replace "blind obedience" with the practice of seeking to create well-being. "Jesus," she maintained, "did not conceive of the world according to a model of completed order, which persons were merely required to maintain. The world he entered had not yet reached perfection. It was alterable, in fact, it awaited transformation."[43] The need for transformation of the world is no less in our day, and the qualities of imagination and creativity are as much in demand as ever. And because grace builds on nature, Christians can learn much from what psychologists and educators have discovered about the nature of creativity and the creative process.

II

CREATIVITY AND THE CREATIVE PROCESS

What do we mean when we say a person is "creative"? Do we reserve the term for artists and geniuses? The evidence from research suggests we should not. Scientific investigation of creativity got a special boost in 1950 when J. P. Guilford devoted his presidential address to the American Psychological Association to creativity, and since then many psychologists and educational theorists have concluded that creativity is a universal human ability, though its expression varies widely in degree and in kind.[44] As the eminent educator E. Paul Torrance has written, "Creative abilities are inherited to the extent that a person inherits his sense organs, a peripheral nervous system, and a brain. How these abilities develop and function, however, is strongly influenced by the way the environment responds to a person's curiosity and creative needs."[45]

At a minimum, creativity involves bringing something new, original, and valuable to a situation. It is certainly basic to the arts, but it also shows itself in science, theology, and other domains of culture, as well as in everyday situations from writing a term paper to planning a party. Theorists make a useful distinction between everyday, personal creativity and the more eminent, exceptional creativity that is associated with individuals who have transformed a discipline or changed the course of history. I would not press this distinction too far, however, because the creative process is similar for both types, and how eminent or exceptional a contribution will prove to be is something that we cannot know in advance. Moreover, much that we have learned about everyday creativity has come from studies of famous creative persons, such as those conducted by Donald MacKinnon at Berkeley in the 1950s and by Mihaly Csickszentmihalyi at the University of Chicago in the 1990s. Among the ninety-one eminently creative individuals interviewed for the latter project were the Nobel Prize–winning novelist Nadine Gordimer, the founder of Citizens for Clean Air Hazel Henderson, the Newberry Award winner Madeleine L'Engle, the poets May Sarton and Denise Levertov, and the recipient of the Nobel Prize in Physiology and Medicine, Rosalyn Yalow.[46]

I have long appreciated MacKinnon's observations on what he calls the "briefcase syndrome of creativity":

One of the most striking observations we have made [in our study of highly effective individuals] is that

the creative person seldom fits the layman's stereotype of him. In our experience, he is not the emo-
tionally unstable, sloppy, loose-jointed Bohemian...
[of popular imagination. Instead,] we discover ourselves using such adjectives as deliberate, reserved,
industrious, and thorough to describe truly original
and creative persons....The truly creative individual
has an image of himself as a responsible person and
a sense of destiny about himself as a human being.[47]

MacKinnon's observations were made more than
forty years ago, and they catalyzed for me then the
sense that creativity and ethics are linked through
this notion of responsibility. When I had the
opportunity in graduate school to investigate this
link, I turned first to the writings of Russian
philosopher Nicolas Berdyaev, who had a chapter
on "The Ethics of Creativeness" in his ethical
study from 1931, *The Destiny of Man*. I have
always appreciated the way Berdyaev grounded
his ethics in a religious response to the mystery of
existence. "I still believe," he wrote in 1916, "that
God calls men to creative activity and to a creative
answer to His love. Our creativeness should be the
expression of our love toward God."[48]

Berdyaev's emphasis on an ethics of creativeness
derived from a theological understanding that
regarded "man" as the image of God the Creator,
stressed the presence and activity of the Holy Spirit,
and interpreted the New Testament as emphasizing

the call to creative service. Unfortunately, however, when Berdyaev said "man," he thought primarily about "the male human being," unlike those writers who thought more broadly and only expressed themselves in what we now call the "generic masculine." Indeed, Berdyaev's philosophy of creativeness was deeply flawed by his belief in gender essentialism, as, for example, when he wrote, "The masculine element is essentially creative and the feminine birth-giving. But neither in generation nor in creativeness can the masculine and the feminine principles be isolated; they interact and complete one another. Woman inspires man to create."[49] Although Berdyaev acknowledged that women's generativity is not limited to physical birth-giving, and although he held up the ideal of "androgynous wholeness," it is clear that for him women have distinct gifts and responsibilities and operate in a much more narrowly determined sphere than do men. For him, woman's essence is to be a mother, whether literally or in a spiritual fashion. She is *not* destined to be a creator.

The gender bias of Berdyaev and others needed to be challenged, and it was encouraging to find psychologist Abraham Maslow observe in a 1962 paper that "we cannot study creativeness in an ultimate sense until we realize that practically all the definitions that we have been using of creativeness, and most of the examples of creativeness that we use, are essentially male or male or masculine products."[50] Also in the 1960s, the educator E. Paul Torrance noted that "boys and girls in different ways suffer in creative development from society's misplaced emphasis on sex role differences."[51] This insight influenced me profoundly when I encountered it, and contributed to my growing feminist consciousness in the 1960s.

It would take the Women's Movement and the development of women's studies to begin to address some of these problems, and although progress has been made there is still work to be done. Even in the 1990s, when psychologist Mihaly Csikszentmihalyi set out to conduct a study of eminently creative individuals, he was left with a sample of some ninety-one persons, of whom about 70 percent were male. "The same percentage of women and men accepted [agreed to participate in the study]," he noted, "but since in certain domains well-known creative women are underrepresented, we were unable to achieve the fifty-fifty gender ratio we were hoping for."[52] This result was likely related to his decision to focus on individuals over age sixty, who had "made a difference to a major domain of culture—one of the sciences, the arts, business, government, or human well-being in general."[53] Had he lowered the age limit, the study might have been more balanced. Still it is encouraging that Csikszentmihalyi had at least wanted a more balanced study, and that his interpretation of gender differences is not based on essentialism. He writes: "Within any given discipline women will use mental processes similar to those men use to reach creative results, but the differences in socialization, training, and opportunities available to men and women in a given social system may impact on the frequency and kind of creative contributions made by the two genders."[54]

What, then, are these mental processes about which he writes? Experts have varied in certain details as they delineate "the creative process," but some features are constant and, significantly, they apply to different kinds of activities, from organizing a conference to writing a novel, designing a car that gets one hundred miles to the gallon, or deciding how to handle a moral dilemma. I offer here a list of eight steps in the creative process, which combines ideas from Csikszentmihalyi's 1996 volume *Creativity* and a 1968 work by Don Fabun, *You and Creativity*.[55] Before discussing the list, however, I would stress Csikszentmihalyi's insight that "the creative process is less linear than recursive," by which he means that the steps are not usually followed in a neat order of progression, but often circle back and repeat themselves at different points in the process.[56] This will become clearer as I describe the eight steps, or stages, in the creative process: desire, preparation, manipulation, incubation, intimation, insight, evaluation, and elaboration.

1. *Desire*. On Fabun's list the first stage of the creative process is the desire to accomplish the cre-

ative deed. Perhaps this will involve a blend of extrinsic and intrinsic motives. At first we may desire to write a dissertation or senior thesis in order to graduate and get on with life, but ideally the topic selected will capture our attention and entice us to enjoy the labor required for completing the work. Creative behavior is often described as problem-solving behavior, and persons who exhibit a high degree of creativity will typically set problems for themselves, sometimes ones that engage them for a lifetime. What keeps desire alive over the course of weeks, months, or years? Here Csikszentmihalyi's famous concept of "flow" can be helpful. Flow is the psychological state we experience when our talents are fully engaged and our attention is entirely focused on the activity at hand. We may know it when reading, playing tennis, composing a letter, or painting a picture. The theory of flow assumes that the mind's natural state is chaotic and unfocused, and thus we are easily bored, anxious, or depressed. To understand flow, picture a two-dimensional grid where a base line represents a situation that presents no challenges to our abilities, and where as a result we feel bored. Then imagine a vertical line representing challenges that exceed our abilities—composing a substantial essay in ten minutes, for example—and the feeling is one of anxiety. Now imagine a diagonal line that slopes up from the corner where the base and the vertical lines meet.

Along that diagonal, where our talents are fully engaged but not unreasonably taxed, is the experience of flow. As Csikszentmihalyi puts it, "…in flow it is clear what has to be done, and our skills are potentially adequate to the challenges."[57] We are so involved in the activity that we lose track of everything else, including time. We are "in the moment," and it is a pleasurable experience.

As our talents develop, we will seek greater challenges that enhance the pleasure of discovery and novelty in the activities that give us the experience of flow. We will want to play in an intermediate tennis league, or try to complete a Sudoku puzzle with three stars, or compose an opera. We will crave with all our hearts a way to give women greater voice in the church, or to reduce the incidence of gun violence, or to improve the health care system. The pleasure of flow is inextricably tied to the struggle to achieve something difficult; it is not a matter of easy satisfaction. We also need to recognize that in order to experience flow, we must focus on the task at hand, so it will be necessary to discipline our desires as well as to kindle them. We cannot work on everything at once. Our brain can hold only so much information in consciousness at one time, and multitasking tends to have diminishing returns.

Finally, to the eyes of faith, the pleasurable experiences associated with devoting our talents to challenging projects can be seen as an experience of God, acknowledging that an experience of God is always also at the same time an experience of something else, and remembering Augustine's wisdom about human desire being ultimately the desire for God. In Csikszentmihalyi's study of eminently creative persons, he found that "what kept them motivated was the quality of experience they felt when they were involved with the activity."[58] Desire, this first step, is not always mentioned in descriptions of the creative process, but I believe it is crucial, for the process must start here. And the creatively responsible moral agent will return again and again to the values and concerns that motivate her to desire a solution to the problem calling for her response.

2. *Preparation.* This step can be considered both in terms of the remote preparation that readies an individual for a particular project through specialized study or years of practice, and the immediate preparation she undertakes once she comes to focus on a specific problem or creative task. In the latter sense, preparation may involve research, reading, assembling materials, and, as Csikszentmihalyi relates, "becoming immersed, consciously or not, in a set of problematic issues that are interesting and arouse curiosity."[59] Although creative insight involves novelty and divergent, or unusual, thinking, a good measure of knowledge and what psychologists term "convergent" thinking will also be needed for the later steps of the process.[60] This is what motivates creative individuals to spend time at this

preparatory stage and to return to this stage later on when necessary. For writers it is always a challenge to know when sufficient research has been done and the drafting process can begin; sometimes people are stuck at this stage out of fear, as was the case with George Eliot's character Edmund Casaubon of *Middlemarch*, who had boxes full of research for his *Key to All Mythologies* but could not bring himself to begin writing the book.[61]

3. *Manipulation*. This third step involves playing with the ideas and possibilities that have begun to emerge from preparatory work. Brainstorming the strategies for solving a problem, sketching out possible structures for what one will build, or contemplating which media or colors to employ may be done at this time. Many lists and sketches will end up on the cutting-room floor. Sometimes it becomes clear that one must do more preparation for a facet of what is emerging. At this stage it is important to let the imagination have free range and not to impose critical objections too quickly.

4. *Incubation*. This is the paradoxical stage, where the mind does not focus directly on solving the problem or designing the structure, but rather is receptive to solutions and ideas that present themselves seemingly without effort on our part. As Csikszentmihalyi notes, during this stage "ideas churn around below the threshold of consciousness," and "unusual connections are likely to be made" that are not the result of our linear,

logical efforts.[62] Really productive ideas, however, tend to come to well-prepared minds, and incubation involves resting *after* effort, not without having made it. Arthur Cropley has emphasized the importance of knowledge and convergent thinking to the creative process, declaring that knowledge is "the basis of intuition" and quoting Louis Pasteur's famous remark, "Chance favors only the prepared mind." He contrasts Antoine Becquerel's discovery of radiation in 1896 with Eugen Semmer's failure to appreciate the curative potential of penicillin in 1870 to illustrate this point. Because Becquerel had the knowledge and research skills to appreciate the fact that the fogging of a photographic plate that had been left in a drawer with some uranium was significant, he went on to investigate the phenomenon and is credited with discovering radioactivity, receiving the Nobel Prize in Physics with Marie and Pierre Curie in 1903. Semmer, however, merely reported that two ill horses he had expected to die recovered, to his surprise, after exposure to spores of *Penicillium notatum*, thus frustrating his efforts to complete pathology reports on them. He missed entirely the curative potential of the fungus that had "ruined" his pathology project, a fact that Cropley attributes to his narrow focus of awareness and interest.[63]

5. *Intimation*. This brief stage involves the sense that a solution is about to emerge. Here one feels

a glimmer of possibility rather than seeing a full plan for the solution, but the feeling can be welcomed in the hope that the sixth stage is just around the corner.

6. *Insight*. Here one is given the solution to the problem, the idea that allows one to make the work, resolve the difficulty, or at least begin to do so. This is the "aha" experience, the moment when things have gelled into a new and promising pattern. Csikszentmihalyi offers a vivid description on the basis of his interviews with eminently creative persons: "The insight presumably occurs when a subconscious connection between ideas fits so well that it is forced to pop out into awareness, like a cork held underwater breaking out into the air after it is released."[64] For instance, an architect might suddenly realize that more light and air will be available if a building is turned 90 degrees from what had originally been planned, or a playwright might find just the right metaphor to unify the scenes she already has begun to sketch, as when Ntozake Shange came up with the title for her choreopoem *for colored girls who have considered suicide when the rainbow is enuf*. The rainbow symbol unifies the various stories in this play not only by accounting for the characters, who dress in colors for their names ("lady in blue," "lady in red," etc.), but also by connecting the theme of hope in the midst of suffering with the biblical sign of God's covenant with Noah.[65]

7. *Evaluation*. The insight, of course, must be assessed. As Csikszentmihalyi describes: "The painter steps back from the canvas to see whether the composition works, the poet rereads the verse with a more critical eye, the scientist sits down to do the calculations or run the experiments."[66] It is here that the knowledge gained in the preparation stage comes into play. In the cold light of day, some ideas do not pan out. But those that still show promise deserve to be tested further in the final step, verification or elaboration.

8. *Elaboration*. This can be a tedious part of the process, involving work that is often slow and routine. Csikszentmihalyi calls this the "99% Perspiration" phase, borrowing from Thomas Edison's observation that genius is 1 percent inspiration and 99 percent perspiration. At this stage it is important to focus on the work in progress while being open to new ideas and staying in touch with the feelings that motivated one to undertake the project in the first place. Csikszentmihalyi quotes at length from Natalie Davis, the historian and author of *The Return of Martin Guerre*, about her feelings at this last stage, when she is ready to write up the findings of her research. She stresses the need to keep desire alive and also communicates how she experiences the recursive nature of the process, the fact that these eight steps do not proceed in linear fashion but circle back and repeat themselves over and over again. Davis observes:

If I didn't have affect in a project, if I had lost it or maybe it didn't last too long, it would lose its spark. I mean, I don't want to do something that I have lost my love for....It is hard to be creative if you are just doing something doggedly. If I didn't have curiosity, if I felt that my curiosity was limited, then the novelty part of it would be gone. Because it is the curiosity that has often pushed me to think of ways of finding out about something that people thought you could never find out about. Or ways of looking at a subject that have never been looked at before. That's what keeps me running back and forth to the library, and just thinking, and thinking, and thinking.[67]

During the elaboration phase it is also necessary to pay attention to the situation to which one wants to contribute the creative insight or product. This reality check is necessary to ensure that the novelty will have some chance of "making it" in the world beyond one's study or laboratory.

Here it will be useful to draw the distinction between "everyday" and "eminent" creativity more explicitly, for the situations affected by the creative process vary significantly according to type. Psychologist Ruth Richards has characterized everyday creativity as a "survival capability," the originality demanded by the changing environments of ordinary life that lead us to "improvise," "flexibly adapt," and "try this and that." We employ everyday creativity in matters such as "making a living, raising a child, feeding the family, writing a report, or finding our way out of the woods when lost."[68] Mihaly Csikszentmihalyi acknowledges the reality of this sort of creativity at the personal level, but has focused his research on what he calls "creativity with a capital C," which is distinguished by the fact that it has left its mark on some aspect of culture. He takes a social and systemic approach to the phenomenon of creativity, arguing that eminent creativity, or "creativity with a capital C," involves the interrelationship among three components: a domain, a field, and an individual. Csikszentmihalyi's attention to the social and institutional aspects of creativity is instructive for anyone who hopes to influence culture or help make the world a better place. By *domain* he means "a set of symbolic rules and procedures," such as those involved in music, chemistry, or mathematics. By *field* he is referring to the experts in the domain, who serve as "gatekeepers" for deciding which original ideas deserve to be welcomed into the domain. For example, in the domain of visual arts, the field is comprised of teachers, curators, collectors, critics, and others who judge which "new works of art deserve to be recognized, preserved, and remembered."[69] In the domain of Catholic moral theology, the field includes experts trained in Christian theology and ethics and the hierarchy of the church. Disputes in the domain should not surprise us, then, since the training and selection

47

process for gatekeepers varies widely according to institutional context. There are, in short, different criteria for tenuring professors and selecting bishops.

The third component in the system of eminent creativity is the individual person. According to this theory, eminent

> creativity occurs when a person, using the symbols of a given domain such as music, engineering, business, or mathematics, has a new idea or sees a new pattern, and when this novelty is selected by the appropriate field for inclusion into the relevant domain. The next generation will encounter that novelty as part of the domain they are exposed to, and if they are creative, they in turn will change it further. Occasionally creativity involves the establishment of a new domain.[70]

Thus we may get a new discipline, such as biochemistry or computer science, as a result. Csikszentmihalyi's theory sets a high bar for creativity, and it focuses on Nobel laureates and famous writers more than on ordinary individuals. Nevertheless, his attention to the social and institutional dimensions of creativity is instructive for everyone, and I believe it has special relevance for *women* seeking to influence one or another domain of human culture, especially domains whose gatekeepers are male. I have in mind especially the domain of religion, and more precisely the domain of Catholicism. It is at this point that my thoughts turn to conscience because this term bears directly on the tension experienced by Catholics who seek to change certain of the church's teachings and practices affecting women.

III

CONSCIENCE AS A CONTESTED TERM

History teaches us that religious traditions do change and develop over time, and this has certainly been the case with Catholicism. Novelty has been introduced by creative minds at critical junctures over the centuries, and has at times been welcomed by the gatekeepers, as when the Council of Nicea affirmed the nonbiblical term *homoousios* to describe the consubstantiality of the first and second Persons of the Trinity, and when the Second Vatican Council endorsed the modern concept of religious freedom. Catholic moral teaching has developed, too, as John Noonan's 2005 study *A Church That Can and Cannot Change* has shown, with special attention to the case of slavery.[71] It is no secret that pressures for change are being felt within the Catholic Church today on a number of moral questions, particularly concerning sexuality, and that Catholic women are inclined to differ with certain magisterial teachings more greatly than men, although male rates of dissent on these questions are also considerable. The 2007 volume by sociologists William V. D'Antonio and his colleagues, *American Catholics Today: New Realities of Their Faith and Their Church*, compares data from earlier studies and concludes that there has been an increasing trend for Catholics of both sexes to see the individual rather than church leaders as the "proper locus of moral authority" on questions such as divorce and remarriage, contraception, homosexual behavior, and nonmarital sex. They note that "Catholics have increasingly seen authority in individual consciences," while their reliance on church leaders for moral wisdom on these matters has declined.[72]

But what is this "conscience" that is said to serve as the locus of individual authority? The term is often used unthinkingly, and its meaning can vary widely. Some ethicists have analyzed several types and distinctions with respect to conscience, while others prefer to avoid the term *conscience* altogether because they believe different words can convey more precisely what is meant. In saying that *conscience* is a contested term, I am claiming both that its meaning is disputed and that the word itself has come to represent a situation of impasse between the hierarchy and many Catholics, a stalemate in a struggle to determine whether and to what extent new ethical ideas should influence church life and teaching.

I am of the school that believes it is better to analyze and employ the term *conscience* with care than to try to change linguistic habits that have been entrenched for centuries. In my book *Liberating Conscience* I developed a social theory of conscience that takes account of the paradox that, although conscience is an individual religious experience, one's personal sense of obligation before God is reached and held in the presence of a community of accountability. I argued against absolutizing the autonomy of conscience and critiqued metaphors implying that conscience is some sort of "thing," like a piece of moral radar equipment that allows one to home in on the right deed like a plane landing in a fog. Instead, I argued, conscience is an aspect of the self, perhaps on a par with intelligence. We all have some of it, but degrees vary greatly, and even a lot of it is no guarantee we will always be right. I defined conscience as personal moral awareness, experienced in the course of anticipating future situations and making moral decisions as well as in the process of reflecting on past decisions and the quality of one's character. This led me to affirm the value of church teaching authority, the legitimacy of dissent, the importance of personal responsibility, and the need for the privileged to listen to voices from the margins.[73]

Since completing that study some years ago I have continued to analyze the rhetoric of conscience, and though I am far from declaring a moratorium on the term, I now think there is one phrase about conscience we might profitably question and perhaps even abstain from using for a while. The phrase is found in official church literature as well as in popular writing on moral education, and it is not a bad phrase in itself, but I believe we stand to gain if, for a while, we stopped speaking of the "formation of conscience." Why do I say this? Much of the rhetoric of conscience gives the impression that the reality to which it refers is either *different* from the self ("the voice of God") or a sort of *thing* within the self, like the moral radar equipment that I mentioned. And so, to avoid this tendency to reify and separate conscience from the moral agent by implying that shaping the radar dish and plugging in the right wires, as it were, is what moral education is all about, I suggest that when we are inclined to use the phrase "formation of conscience" we would do well to stop and think, and maybe say something else. What about saying, for example, the "formation of the moral agent," or even better, the "formation of the creatively responsible moral agent"?

IV

CONSCIENCE AS THE CREATIVELY RESPONSIBLE SELF

In the aftermath of World War II the term *responsibility* became prominent in Christian ethics, as thinkers such as Bernard Häring, Dietrich Bonhoeffer, and H. Richard Niebuhr sought to overcome the emphasis on duty and obedience that had dominated ethical reflection prior to the Nuremburg trials, when ex-Nazis tried to defend their atrocities on grounds of "following orders."[74] Niebuhr's book *The Responsible Self* is a profound philosophical essay on moral agency, which I still find an inspiring description of much that the experience of conscience involves.[75] Further research has convinced me, however, that we do well to distinguish two ways of being responsible, one that is more passive and the other more creative. The former involves fulfilling the commonly recognized duties of one's state in life, while the latter looks beyond the immediate obligations of commandments and social roles and seeks to contribute in new ways to the contexts of one's life, striving to accomplish good on a wider scale, and thus "bearing fruit for the life of the world" (*Optatam Totius*, no. 16).

We might in fact interpret the story of Jesus and the rich young man who kept the commandments but could not risk leaving his goods to follow the imaginative teacher and healer to new endeavors (Matt 19) as voicing the desire of Jesus for disciples whose ethical ideals extend beyond conforming to law and social expectations, notwithstanding their importance. "If you wish to enter into life," Jesus tells the young man, "keep the commandments," and after having done that, "if you wish to be perfect, go, sell your possessions, and give the money to the poor, and you will have treasure in heaven; then come, follow me" (vv. 16–22). The Gospel itself interprets this story as mainly concerning the danger of riches, and in subsequent centuries many Christians have interpreted the invitation to perfection as having to do with a vocation to the religious life with its vow of poverty. I believe, however, that this narrative can, in addition, be read as supporting an ethic that involves both appropriate conformity to law and duty and also a willingness to take appropriate risks and attempt new things that will make our love of neighbor a truly efficacious one.

Responsibility's passive dimension has been greatly stressed in Catholic literature, whereas there has been much less emphasis on creative responsibility, which involves the ability to think independently and to take risks for the sake of helping to improve life for oneself and one's neighbors. Both types of responsibility are needed, like the black and white keys on the piano. The problem is that socialization has equipped many of us too well for the one, and very poorly for the other. Women and men alike have received moral training that denies or minimizes the agent's role in recognizing obligations and in balancing obligations that conflict. Many women, however, face particular challenges insofar as the socialization of females has tended to foster passivity and stifle growth toward exercising power and original thinking.[76]

And yet we do have many instances of women who have exercised creative responsibility. Dorothy Day, cofounder with Peter Maurin of the Catholic Worker Movement, comes to mind, as does Mother Alfred Moes, OSF, a key figure in the founding of the Mayo Clinic. After a tornado had devastated the frontier town of Rochester, Minnesota, in 1883, this community leader persuaded Dr. William W. Mayo to staff a hospital if she would build it. With the support of her religious community she could deliver on this promise, and she raised enough funds to open St. Mary's Hospital in 1889. In 1894 Dr. Mayo testified to the importance of her initiative, for he had at first been reluctant to change his medical practice. Speaking of the conversation that led to the hospital, he observed:

...the Mother Superior came down to my office and in the course of the visit she asked, "Doctor, do you not think a hospital in this city would be an excellent thing?" I answered, "Mother Superior, this city is too small to support a hospital." I told her that the erection of a hospital was a difficult undertaking and required a great deal of money, and moreover we had no assurance of its success even after a great deal of time and money had been put into it. "Very well," she persisted, "but you just promise me to take charge of it and we will set that building before you at once. With our faith and hope and energy, it will succeed."[77]

There is a gospel parable that can encourage us to emulate such women as Mother Alfred Moes and to become more creatively responsible selves. This is the Parable of the Talents from Matthew's Gospel (25:14–30). This story immediately precedes the narrative of the Last Judgment (25:31–46), in which Jesus rewards the faithful with the words, "I was hungry and you gave me food, I was thirsty and you gave me drink" (v. 35a). In the Parable of the Talents, three servants are given different sums of money as their master departs for a trip. The servant who received the least amount buried his money out of fear. The other two servants risked investing their talents, and their money doubled in value. In the end these creatively responsible servants are rewarded, while the timid, fearful servant does not fare so well. This fearful servant reminds me of someone who sees the moral life only as a matter of not breaking the rules. And we might interpret the difference between the two and the five talents as symbolizing the different levels of creative responsibility, what Csikszentmihalyi distinguishes as everyday personal creativity, or creativity with a lowercase *c*, and eminent or culture-changing creativity, demarcated by an uppercase *C*.

My grandmother, Stella Farrell Flynn, was probably closer to the lowercase form of creativity when she found a way to feed her eleven children during the Depression of the 1930s, and still had something for the unemployed men who came to their kitchen door hungry. Dorothy Day, on the other hand, is recognized as having made a lasting change in Catholic and urban culture, and Csikszentmihalyi would regard her as eminently creative. Like Dorothy Day and Mother Alfred Moes, Sister Madeleva is another instance of eminent creativity, and her life also helps us appreciate the way creative responsibility is related to institutional and social life, or "domains" and "fields," as Csikszentmihalyi calls them.

Madeleva's personal creativity showed itself in many ways—her poetry, her teaching, her correspondence, her essays, and her autobiographical writings, to mention a few. To my knowledge, however, she did not introduce lasting novelty into the domains of literature or pedagogy, so that we can say they will never be the same as a result of her efforts. But I think we can say that her creativity with respect to the Sister Formation Movement and the School of Sacred Theology at Saint Mary's College was of the eminent or culture-changing variety.

What she catalyzed with her efforts to ensure that teaching sisters received professional training before being sent into the classroom has had an enormous and lasting impact, not only on the religious congregations involved but on American Catholic culture as a whole. In her 1997 biography of Madeleva, Gail Porter Mandell stresses the importance of a panel she had organized for the National Catholic Education Association in 1949, which included groundbreaking papers by Madeleva and several others that were later published under the title *The Education of Sister Lucy*.[78] Three years later, Mandell notes, the first national gathering of U.S. religious took place in August 1952 at the University of Notre Dame, and this "formed the link between the ideas published in *The Education of Sister Lucy* and the actual Sister Formation program, established in 1954."[79]

Likewise the innovation of opening Saint Mary's School of Sacred Theology in 1943, which had resulted from Madeleva's interest in providing education for teachers of religion, was of the culture-changing variety. Today we tend to forget how dramatic a change it was when women first gained the credentials for teaching theology at the college and graduate levels, but it was the program started by Madeleva that first made it possible for nonclerics to earn graduate degrees in Catholic theology. According to the 1982 directory of the Catholic Theological Society of America, all the women members with PhD degrees from the 1950s had studied at Saint Mary's College. Among them was Margaret Brennan, IHM, who earned her doctorate in 1953, and later, as leader of her congregation, systematically encouraged younger sisters, including Madeleva Lecturers Sandra M. Schneiders, IHM, and Mary Ann Hinsdale, IHM, to pursue advanced studies in theology.[80] Besides her work in community administration, which included service as president of the national Leadership Conference of Women Religious in 1972, Brennan taught numerous graduate students during twenty-five years as a professor of pastoral theology at Regis College of the University of Toronto.[81] Another eminent graduate of Saint Mary's School of Sacred Theology was Mary Anthony Wagner, OSB, who completed her PhD in 1957 and taught theology at the College of St. Benedict and St. John's University in Minnesota for thirty-seven years. With Paschal Botz, OSB, she cofounded the Benedictine Institute of Sacred Theology there for nonclerics and was associate dean for ten years. In 1974 this institute merged with the seminary at St. John's to become St. John's University School of Theology, and Wagner was its first dean, serving until 1978. She later edited the national publication *Sisters Today* from 1979 until its last issue in November 2000.

At the fortieth anniversary meeting of the College Theology Society in 1994, M. Shawn Copeland declared in a plenary address:

> By inserting women into the stream of academic theology, [Madeleva] laid the condition of the possibility of a distinctive theological contribution emerging from women's reflection on our particular human, religious, cultural, political, and economic experiences in light of the Word of God....Because of her labor, Roman Catholic women have been engaged in the study and practice of theology now for fifty years.[82]

In sum, the School of Sacred Theology at Saint Mary's College has had a profound effect on the discipline of Christian theology and arguably on global Christianity as well.

Both these influential efforts illustrate the social-institutional side of creativity. We might suppose that the School of Sacred Theology and the Sister Formation Movement were sudden inspirations that came from nowhere to Madeleva's convent room, perhaps as she was writing a poem or tying her shoelaces. But the process was more complex, as Mandell's biography makes clear, and it was much more *social* than the stereotype of the solitary creative genius suggests. In terms of the creative process, Madeleva had greatly desired to improve religious education and do better justice to the talents of women religious; she had done considerable preparatory work before coming up with her remarkably productive ideas; and the issues were incubating as she went about other tasks and talked with her friends. The insights may seem to have come suddenly, but they came to a well-prepared mind and to a moral agent who knew how to engage others in effecting change for the good.

With respect to the School of Sacred Theology, Mandell shows that Madeleva's creativity here depended very much on her social life and her involvement with the Holy Cross Sisters, the National Catholic Education Association (NCEA), and church leaders. By the early 1940s Madeleva had long deplored the quality of religious education in Catholic schools, but it took a remark by her friend Frank Sheed about the fact that nowhere in the country could a layperson do graduate studies in theology to give her the idea that something practical might be done about the problem. And when her requests to Catholic University, Notre Dame, Marquette, and other universities to admit nonclerics to their graduate theology programs were turned down, she mentioned this disappointment to the head of the bishops' committee on the Confraternity of Christian Doctrine, Bishop Edwin O'Hara, while he was visiting Saint Mary's, and it was *he* who suggested that she might start something on her own campus. Mandell reports:

> At the time [Madeleva] demurred, fearful of what she described as "presumption." At the next meeting of the NCEA, with all other possibilities exhausted, she responded to "a strange impulse outside [her] will." Rising, she announced: "I do not know how we will do it, but this summer [1943] we will offer at Saint Mary's a six weeks' graduate program in Theology....We will send you details in a fortnight."[83]

Madeleva's friends Frank Sheed and Edwin O'Hara had played key roles in this instance of her creativity, and she quickly enlisted others to help with implementing the idea of a School of Sacred Theology. Two Jesuits and a monsignor taught noncredit courses to eighteen sisters from various communities that first summer, and the school was formally established with doctoral- and master's-level programs in place the following year. Madeleva drew on her experience with this school in her contributions to *The Education of Sister Lucy*, arguing in "The Preparation of Teachers of Religion" that Catholic institutions were guilty of heresy if they thought that "any teacher wearing a religious habit can *de facto* teach religion," and asking why Catholic colleges and universities did not invest in theological studies the way they did in science:

We have teachers who can make science and embalmed cats subjects for absorbing study. Will we, and when will we train teachers to make God and the science of theology the supreme subject in our curricula? We have millions of dollars for research in smashing the atom. Will we, and when will we devote our resources to the study of the Power that holds our atoms together?[84]

Saint Mary's School of Sacred Theology flourished for two decades, closing only when Madeleva's earlier goal of having university theology programs available to nonclerics had been achieved. During that time this small program prepared a generation of women theologians and has had an incalculable impact on the church.

Having mentioned some of the contributions of Margaret Brennan, IHM, and Mary Anthony Wagner, OSB, we have only to reel in the chain of causality represented by another graduate, this one from 1954, to reinforce this point about influence. I refer to the theologian-turned-philosopher Mary Daly, who helped launch the Christian feminist movement and its theoretical contributions to Christian theology. If Daly had not earned her doctorate at Saint Mary's College, would she have been motivated to seek further training in Europe so that her theological knowledge would be certified with the same pontifical degree that clerical theologians possessed? Indeed, if she had not studied Thomas Aquinas so assiduously at Saint Mary's College, would she have been able to hold her own as the only female in a sea of cassocked seminarians at the University of Fribourg in Switzerland? We may well wonder whether *The Church and the Second Sex* would have been written, and whether the discussion that ensued in Christian feminist theology would have been delayed or taken a different course.[85] The fact that Daly herself eventually rejected Catholicism and theology testifies to the ambiguous results of creativity, but does not deny either Daly's or Madeleva's participation in culture-changing creativity.

I would note that the quality that led Madeleva to seek new solutions to significant problems can be called the virtue of creativity, insofar as a virtue is a moral excellence, a strength of character that contributes to habitually good action in some respect. As a virtue creativity involves the disposition to step back from a situation of difficulty, look at options imaginatively, and take reasonable risks for the sake of new and better possibilities. Creativity can, of course, be put to evil purposes, and in that case it is not virtuous.[86] And even when creativity is virtuous, its results will not be perfectly good, for under the conditions of finitude, human choices tend to have ambiguous results and unforeseen consequences. Furthermore, not every moral dilemma calls for a "new" response; discernment is needed to ascertain whether conformity or creativity is called for in a given situation, and often conformity is needed. For instance, when the Vatican insisted in the early 1980s that the Sisters of Mercy halt discussions in their hospitals about whether some sterilizations could be allowed, the women leading the community realized that failure to do so would likely cause division in the congregation and ultimately result in harm to their ministry of health care. Although the Mercy leaders did not agree with the Vatican's reasoning, they obeyed its demand for the sake of what they judged to be the greater good under the difficult circumstances they faced.[87]

For all these reasons it may be better to speak of the virtue of creative responsibility than simply creativity, for "creative responsibility" conveys the element of prudence, discernment, and caring as well as imagination. But however we name the quality, the important thing is to cultivate it. And I think we improve the odds of fostering this virtue if we think of moral education in terms of developing creatively responsible selves, rather than as a matter of "forming" some abstraction called "conscience." The investment of talents, whether one or two or five, must happen with the awareness that one cannot fully predict the results of a deed undertaken in the hope of doing good. But the Parable of the Talents from Matthew's Gospel makes clear that the willingness to take reasonable risks in responsibility before our Creator should characterize the person of faith.

The need for creative responsibility is evident in so many of the moral dilemmas we face on a daily basis. Take the case featured in the *Hastings Center Report* in late 2008, concerning a doctor and a nurse who seek to treat an immigrant woman from Sudan who tests positive for HIV. This woman, named Alna, speaks very little English and has mainly pointed at pictures to communicate with clinic workers, but she refuses to allow a translator into the room because she fears her HIV status will become known in the small immigrant community. Very likely Alna contracted the virus from her husband, and she is afraid of violence from him and separation from their children if her condition should become known. Yet the medical staff feels the obligation to treat Alna, and both doctor and nurse are frustrated by her unwillingness to admit an interpreter. The doctor puts the dilemma thus: "How can we treat her if we can't communicate with her, and how can we communicate with her without an interpreter? She needs HAART (highly active antiretroviral therapy), but for that to be effective, we need to help her understand how important it is to adhere to the prescription regimen to keep the viral load low. Without an interpreter, our hands are tied."[88]

When considered narrowly, this case might seem to be a matter of weighing the ethical principle of beneficence, and in particular the doctor's duty to care for a patient, against the principle of patient autonomy, and concluding either that Alna must be sent home untreated or else subjected to an interview in the presence of a Sudanese translator. But the ethicists who commented on the case for the *Report* took a much broader and more imaginative approach to the dilemma, one that invites the health care professionals to see the problem from Alna's perspective and assist her in providing for her own welfare within a context that is very different from their own. As commentator Christy Rentmeester put it, "Caring competently for Alna means more than just getting her the right prescriptions and monitoring her viral loads; it means making her feel confident that her caregivers understand what's at stake for her and partnering with her to figure out how to integrate new practices into her life with HIV."[89] On a practical level, commentator Dayle DeLancey suggests that this may mean spending some time with the translator when Alna is not there, and also seeking advice from "other local representatives of her culture" about how they might provide truly effective care for Alna.[90]

This case illustrates the need for creative responsibility because the imposition of a translator and even the "gold standard" of highly activated antiretroviral therapy may not be truly life-giving for Alna in her situation. There is at a minimum a need for a *new* approach to the prob-

lem, and this need calls on the creative imaginations of the moral agents involved. I would go so
far as to say it calls for them to exercise a *virtue* of
creative responsibility, a virtue that includes the
ability to take the problem apart, consider it from
different angles, and look for a solution beyond
the impasse originally presented.

Creative responsibility on a larger scale is called
for in Daniel Finn's discussion of "morality in the
marketplace" in the March 2009 issue of *U.S.
Catholic*, especially in light of the economic crisis
then affecting the global economy. In the current
economy, Finn maintains, we cannot simply "leg-
islate a just wage" in the United States, because in
a global economy "to insist that everybody is paid
$11.50 or $13.50 an hour may doom a corpora-
tion." Rather, he observes, "in a market economy,
we have to find new ways to implement the values
protected by the just wage doctrine."[91] Again,
something *new* is needed, and thus creativity is
required. Unfortunately, moral agents trained to
think only in terms of conformity to principles are
not well equipped for the imaginative work
needed to preserve the values that the just wage
doctrine served so well in the past, nor for that
matter to address the new needs for justice that
result from continual innovations in technologies
and business practices around the world.

Finn's call for new approaches to economic justice
reminds me of the story of Jacqueline Novogratz,

with which I opened this book. In seeking to contribute to a better situation for poor people she refused to be content with efforts that felt good subjectively but were not demonstrably effective in catalyzing real improvement. As she gained experience in international banking and microfinance work, she realized that business models that demanded results and accountability had something to offer philanthropists, and eventually she gathered the resources needed to put her ideas about "patient capitalism" to the test and launched the Acumen Fund in 2001. The story of Novogratz also illustrates an aspect of the creatively responsible self I have not mentioned yet, namely, tolerance for long-term involvement with a difficult problem or set of problems. Her creativity had been focused on effective assistance to poor persons for nearly two decades before the Acumen Fund was launched, and even its documented successes have not begun to complete her ambitious agenda. What sustains her in these long-term efforts is the vision of human interdependence she learned in childhood and has seen reinforced in exemplary lives she encountered since then. Quite simply, she is convinced that "we have only one world for all of us on earth, and the future really is ours to create, in a world we dare to imagine together."[92] And although the form of her commitment is very different from that of the saints depicted on the holy cards she received from Sister Mary Theophane in first grade, I believe those cards taught her to aspire to a life that was about much more than observing basic commandments and conforming to societal expectations.

The theologian Bernard Häring understood God to be seeking a creative response from human persons, and argued against moral formation that so emphasizes "literal obedience to static, inflexible norms" that well-intentioned persons "lack the power to see opportunities for doing good above and beyond the law."[93] By contrast, he pointed out, the Christian should learn from the lives of saints, whether canonized or not, that conscience is "the eye of love that discerned new paths toward the historical realization of the kingdom."[94] To be sure, the values of God's realm—love, justice, peace, truth—are never fully realized on Earth, but as baptized persons we are called to use our talents and especially our creativity in their pursuit. What problems of our religious and secular cultures call upon the creativity of each of us for solutions today? To what new paths, I wonder, is the eye of love inviting us?

NOTES

1. Jacqueline Novogratz, *The Blue Sweater: Bridging the Gap between Rich and Poor in an Interconnected World* (New York: Rodale, 2009), 4. Novogratz notes on the copyright page that her memoir employs some pseudonyms.

2. Ibid., iii.

3. Ibid., 251.

4. Ibid., 3.

5. Ibid., 192. For more information, see Anne Field, "Investor in the World's Poor," *Stanford Business Magazine* (May 2007), http://www.gsb.stanford.edu/NEWS/bmag/sbsm0705/feature_novogratz (accessed January 31, 2010).

6. Novogratz, *The Blue Sweater*, 204.

7. Ibid., 208.

8. Ibid., 200.

9. Ibid., 252–53.

10. Ibid., 253.

11. Ibid., 253–54.

12. *Optatam Totius* (#16), "Decree on Priestly Formation," quoted here from Walter M. Abbott, ed., *The Documents of Vatican II* (New York: The America Press, 1966), 452.

13. Monika K. Hellwig, *Christian Women in a Troubled World* (New York: Paulist Press, 1985), 26.

14. Ibid., 54.

15. Dolores R. Leckey, *Women and Creativity* (New York: Paulist Press, 1991).

16. See M. Shawn Copeland, *The Subversive Power of Love: The Vision of Henriette Delille* (New York: Paulist Press, 2009), and, Barbara Fiand, *Awe-Filled Wonder: The Interface of Science and Spirituality* (New York: Paulist Press, 2008), 63–64.

17. Other examples include Elizabeth Johnson's *Women, Earth, and Creator Spirit* (New York: Paulist Press, 1993), which lays a theological foundation for a spirituality and ethics of creativity in its emphasis on the presence of the Divine Creator in our lives, and Margaret Farley's *Compassionate Respect* (New York: Paulist Press, 2002), which stresses the quality of "imaginative attention" to human suffering. More recently, Susan Ross has linked women's creativity with sacramentality in *For the Beauty of the Earth* (New York: Paulist Press, 2006).

18. *Catechism of the Catholic Church*, 2nd ed., #1694 (New York: Doubleday, 1997), 471.

19. William C. Spohn, *Go and Do Likewise: Jesus and Ethics* (New York: Continuum, 1999), 11.

20. NRSV; quoted in Walter Wink, *Jesus and Nonviolence: The Third Way* (Minneapolis: Fortress, 2003), 10.

21. Wink, *Jesus and Nonviolence*, 11.

22. Ibid., 9.

23. Ibid., 15; italics are in the original.

24. Ibid., 16.

25. Ibid., 18.

26. Ibid., 21.

27. Ibid., 24.

28. Ibid., 25.

29. Translation from the Vatican Web site at http://www.vatican.va/archive/hist_councils/ii_vatican_council/documents/vat-ii_const_19651207_gaudium-et-spes_en.html.

30. For current information on these movements, see the Web sites www.romancatholicwomenpriests.org and www.womensordination.org.

31. Wink, *Jesus and Nonviolence*, 27.

32. William C. Spohn, "Jesus and Ethics," *Proceedings of the Catholic Theological Society of America* 49 (1994): 51.

33. Spohn, *Go and Do Likewise*, 49. Bernard Häring had made a similar point in *Free and Faithful in Christ*, vol. 1 (New York: Seabury, 1978), observing that "we look also to the concrete examples of Jesus Christ and his disciples. But we are never stereotypes, nor are the events of our lives carbon copies of earlier times." Rather, imitation that is "guided by His spirit" will have "creative qualities" (22).

34. Spohn, *Go and Do Likewise*, 4.

35. Ibid., 52.

36. Ibid.

37. Ibid., 53.

38. Ibid., 54.

39. Ibid., 56.

40. William C. Spohn, "The Formative Power of Story and the Grace of Indirection," in *Seeking Goodness and Beauty: The Use of the Arts in Theological Ethics*, ed.

Patricia Lamoureux and Kevin J. O'Neill (Lanham, MD: Rowman & Littlefield, 2005), 29.

41. Spohn, *Go and Do Likewise*, 38.

42. Ibid., 161; italics are in the original.

43. Dorothee Soelle, *Beyond Mere Obedience*, trans. Lawrence W. Denef (1968; New York: The Pilgrim Press, 1982), 27. Other studies by Christian ethicists that emphasize imagination and creativity include Bernard Häring, *Free and Faithful in Christ*, vol. 1 (New York: Seabury, 1978); Philip Keane, *Christian Ethics and Imagination* (New York: Paulist Press, 1983); Thomas E. McCollough, *The Moral Imagination and Public Life* (Chatham, NJ: Chatham House, 1991); and Daniel C. Maguire, *The Moral Choice* (Garden City, NY: Doubleday, 1978), *On Moral Grounds* (coauthored with A. Nicholas Fargnoli; New York: Crossroad, 1996), and *Ethics: A Complete Method for Moral Choice* (Minneapolis: Fortress Press, 2010). Also of interest is a special combined issue of the *Creativity Research Journal* 6, nos. 1–2 (1993), which is devoted entirely to "Creativity in the Moral Domain," as well as a more recent essay by Mark A. Runco and Jill Nemiro, "Creativity in the Moral Domain: Integration and Implications," *Creativity Research Journal* 15, no. 1 (2003): 91–105.

44. J. Guilford, "Creativity," *American Psychologist* 5 (1950): 444–54.

45. E. Paul Torrance, "Nurture of Creative Talents," in *Explorations in Creativity*, ed. Ross L. Mooney and Taher A. Razik (New York: Harper & Row, 1967), 185.

46. Mihaly Csikszentmihalyi, *Creativity: Flow and the Psychology of Discovery and Invention* (New York: HarperCollins, 1996), 373–91.

47. Donald W. MacKinnon, "The Highly Effective Individual," in Mooney and Razik, *Explorations in Creativity*, 65.

48. Nicolas Berdyaev, *The Meaning of the Creative Act* (1916), trans. Donald A. Lowrie (New York: Harper and Brothers, 1955), 9.

49. Berdyaev, *The Destiny of Man* (1931), trans. Natalie Duddington (New York: Harper & Row, 1960), 67.

50. Abraham H. Maslow, "The Creative Attitude," in Mooney and Razik, *Explorations in Creativity*, 46.

51. Torrance, "Nurture of Creative Talents," 188.

52. Csikszentmihalyi, *Creativity*, 14.

53. Ibid., 12.

54. Ibid., 405.

55. Don Fabun, *You and Creativity* (Beverly Hills, CA: Glencoe Press, 1968). University of Hamburg professor Arthur Cropley notes that G. Wallas had identified the four stages of preparation, incubation, illumination, and verification in his 1926 volume, *The Art of Thought*, and to these Cropley would add an initial phase of "information" in which the creator becomes aware of the problem and decides to work on it, and two final phases, called "communication" and "validation," in which she presents the results to others and receives appropriate acclaim. See Arthur Cropley, "In Praise of Convergent Thinking," *Creativity Research Journal* 18, no. 3 (2006): 401–2.

56. Csikszentmihalyi, *Creativity*, 80.

57. Ibid., 112.

58. Ibid., 110.

59. Ibid., 79.

60. Cropley stresses the need for a balance of divergent and convergent thinking, arguing that the *effectiveness* of the novelty generated in creative thinking depends to a great extent on logic and knowledge: "I do not intend to deny the importance of divergent thinking in production of effective novelty. However, although necessary, it is not sufficient on its own except perhaps for occasional flukes when blind luck leads to effective novelty. Convergent thinking is necessary, too, because it makes it possible to explore, evaluate, or criticize variability and identify its effective aspects" ("In Praise of Convergent Thinking," 398–99).

61. Eliot's narrator describes Casaubon's mind as "weighted with unpublished matter," and so lost in the details of his research that even if he had been able to overcome his perfectionism and bring himself to write the book, so many years had been lost the findings would have been outdated. See George Eliot, *Middlemarch* (1871–72; New York, Penguin, 1965), 230 and 254.

62. Csikszentmihalyi, *Creativity*, 79.

63. Cropley, "In Praise of Convergent Thinking," 394–95.

64. Csikszentmihalyi, *Creativity*, 104.

65. Ntozake Shange, *for colored girls who have considered suicide when the rainbow is enuf* (1975; New York: Bantam Books, 1980).

66. Csikszentmihalyi, *Creativity*, 104.

67. Ibid., 105.

68. Ruth Richards, ed., "Introduction," in *Everyday Creativity and New Views of Human Nature:*

Psychological, Social, and Spiritual Perspectives (Washington, DC: American Psychological Association, 2007), 3. Although in *Creativity,* Csikszentmihalyi is primarily interested in culture-changing creativity, he concludes his study with a chapter on "Enhancing Personal Creativity" (343–72) that is full of practical suggestions for increasing one's creative energy and productivity in everyday life. Another source of practical advice for enhancing creativity is Julia Cameron's *The Artist's Way: A Spiritual Path to Higher Creativity* (New York: Tarcher/Perigree, 1992).

69. Csikszentmihalyi, *Creativity,* 27–28.

70. Ibid., 28.

71. John T. Noonan, Jr., *A Church That Can and Cannot Change: The Development of Catholic Moral Teaching* (Notre Dame, IN: University of Notre Dame Press, 2005).

72. William V. D'Antonio, James D. Davidson, Dean R. Hoge, and Mary L. Gautier, *American Catholics Today: New Realities of Their Faith and Their Church* (Lanham, MD: Rowman & Littlefield, 2007), 97–98.

73. Anne E. Patrick, *Liberating Conscience: Feminist Explorations in Catholic Moral Theology* (New York: Continuum, 1996), 35–39 and 198–99.

74. Albert R. Jonsen describes this development in *Responsibility in Modern Religious Ethics* (Washington, DC: Corpus Books, 1968).

75. H. Richard Niebuhr, *The Responsible Self: An Essay in Christian Moral Philosophy* (New York: Harper & Row, 1963).

76. I discuss this topic more fully in *Liberating Conscience,* 185–88.

77. See Ellen Whelan, OSF, *The Sisters' Story: Saint Mary's Hospital—Mayo Clinic 1839–1939* (Rochester, MN: Mayo Foundation for Medical Education and Research, 2002), 44. Whelan's chronicle adds that several sisters shared the reluctance initially voiced by Dr. Mayo. The July 1886 record of the sisters' executive council counted twenty-seven votes in favor and four against building the hospital (46).

78. *The Education of Sister Lucy* (Notre Dame: Saint Mary's College, 1949). Madeleva's name is not given as editor, but she had invited the papers and written the opening and concluding essays: "The Education of Our Young Religious Teachers," in which the hypothetical Sister Lucy's educational needs are described (5–10), and "The Preparation of Teachers of Religion in College" (35–39).

79. Gail Porter Mandell, *Madeleva: A Biography* (Albany: State University of New York Press, 1997), 189. See also Karen Kennelly's recent history of the movement, *The Religious Formation Conference 1954–2004* (Silver Spring, MD: Religious Formation Conference, 2009).

80. Sandra M. Schneiders, in addition to being a prolific writer on biblical studies, spirituality, and religious life, has served as president of Society for the Study of Christian Spirituality and also the Catholic Biblical Association of America. Her Madeleva Lectures are *Women and the Word* (New York: Paulist Press, 1986) and *With Oil in Their Lamps: Faith, Feminism, and the Future* (New York: Paulist Press, 2000). Mary Ann Hinsdale was elected vice president of the Catholic Theological Society of America (CTSA)

in 2008, with automatic succession to the presidency in 2010–11. Her Madeleva Lecture, *Women Shaping Theology* (New York: Paulist Press, 2006), mentions (84) that the first two women members of the CTSA, who joined in 1965, were graduates of the doctoral program at Saint Mary's College: Cathleen M. Going (1956) and Elizabeth Farians (1958).

81. See Margaret R. Brennan, IHM, *What Was There for Me Once: A Memoir* (Toronto: Novalis, 2009), and Mary Ellen Sheehan, Mary Heather MacKinnon, and Moni McIntyre, eds., *Light Burdens, Heavy Blessings: Challenges of Church and Culture in the Post Vatican II Era: Essays in Honor of Margaret R. Brennan* (Quincy, IL: Franciscan Press, 2000).

82. M. Shawn Copeland, "Toward a Critical Christian Feminist Theology of Solidarity," in *Women and Theology*, ed. Mary Ann Hinsdale and Phyllis H. Kaminski (Maryknoll, NY: Orbis, 1995), 6.

83. Mandell, *Madeleva*, 185.

84. Madeleva, *The Education of Sister Lucy*, 39.

85. Daly's studies in Europe took place during the Second Vatican Council, and she was inspired by the energy for reform to publish *The Church and the Second Sex* (New York: Harper & Row, 1968). This hopeful, scholarly volume reviewed the history of sexism in the Catholic Church and offered some "modest proposals" for reform. It did not, however, win Daly tenure at Boston College, though that decision was eventually reversed in Daly's favor after student protesters took up her cause. By that time, however, Daly's patience as a Catholic reformer had been exhausted, and, like Martin Luther before her, she grew much more radical. Thus in October 1971, dur-

ing a famous sermon in Harvard Memorial Chapel, she boldly declared Christianity and all patriarchal religions to be morally bankrupt, and urged her followers, women and men, to walk out of the chapel in a symbolic exodus from patriarchy. See Mary Daly, "The Women's Movement: An Exodus Community," *Religious Education* 67 (September–October 1972): 327–33; most of this sermon is reprinted in Elizabeth A. Clark and Herbert Richardson, eds., *Women and Religion: The Original Sourcebook of Women in Christian Thought*, rev. ed. (HarperSanFrancisco, 1996), 311–18. Two years later Daly published *Beyond God the Father: Toward a Philosophy of Women's Liberation* (Boston: Beacon, 1973), a theoretical rejection of Christian theology, whose arguments have since been countered in major works by feminist theologians, including Rosemary Radford Ruether, *Sexism and God Talk: Toward a Feminist Theology* (Boston: Beacon, 1983); Anne E. Carr, *Transforming Grace: Christian Tradition and Women's Experience* (New York: Harper & Row, 1988); and Elizabeth A. Johnson, *She Who Is: The Mystery of God in Feminist Theological Discourse* (New York: Continuum, 1992). Daly has provided autobiographical information in the "New Feminist Postchristian Introduction" to the 1975 edition of *The Church and the Second Sex* (New York: Harper & Row), and also in *Outercourse: The Be-Dazzling Voyage* (HarperSanFrancisco, 1992).

86. See, for example, the special issue of *Creativity Research Journal* 20, no. 2 (2008) on "Malevolent Creativity."

87. I discuss this case more fully in *Liberating Conscience*, 45–48. Earlier, theologian Margaret A.

Farley, a Sister of Mercy, offered an insightful analysis in "Power and Powerlessness: A Case in Point," *CTSA Proceedings* 37 (1982): 116–19, noting that the decision should continue to be reexamined and that the choice of the Sisters of Mercy to remain silent at the time was made in the hope "that theirs and other voices may ultimately prevail." She also acknowledged that there was a danger in the "unfinished story" she had told, namely, "that the silence will grow, and that the power in the Church will be more and more isolated, especially from the experience of women" (119).

88. "Case Study: Trust, Translation, and HAART," with commentaries by Christy A. Rentmeester and Dayle B. DeLancey, *Hastings Center Report* 38 (November–December, 2008): 13.

89. Ibid., 14.

90. Ibid.

91. Daniel Finn, "Can This Market Be Saved?" *U.S. Catholic* (March 2009): 15.

92. Novogratz, *The Blue Sweater*, 254.

93. Bernard Häring, "Building a Creative Conscience," trans. Ingrid Knapp, *Commonweal* (August 11, 1989): 433.

94. Ibid., 435.

The Madeleva Lecture in Spirituality

This series, sponsored by the Center for Spirituality, Saint Mary's College, Notre Dame, Indiana, honors annually the woman who as president of the college inaugurated its pioneering graduate program in theology, Sister M. Madeleva, C.S.C.

1985
Monika K. Hellwig
Christian Women in a Troubled World

1986
Sandra M. Schneiders
Women and the Word

1987
Mary Collins
Women at Prayer

1988
Maria Harris
Women and Teaching

1989
Elizabeth Dreyer
Passionate Women: Two Medieval Mystics

1990
Joan Chittister, OSB
Job's Daughters

1991
Dolores R. Leckey
Women and Creativity

1992
Lisa Sowle Cahill
Women and Sexuality

1993
Elizabeth A. Johnson
Women, Earth, and Creator Spirit

1994
Gail Porter Mandell
Madeleva: One Woman's Life

1995
Diana L. Hayes
Hagar's Daughters

1996
Jeanette Rodriguez
Stories We Live
Cuentos Que Vivimos

1997
Mary C. Boys
Jewish-Christian Dialogue

1998
Kathleen Norris
The Quotidian Mysteries

1999
Denise Lardner Carmody
An Ideal Church: A Meditation

2000
Sandra M. Schneiders
With Oil in Their Lamps

2001
Mary Catherine Hilkert
Speaking with Authority

2002
Margaret A. Farley
Compassionate Respect

2003
Sidney Callahan
Women Who Hear Voices

2004
Mary Ann Hinsdale, IHM
Women Shaping Theology

[No Lecture in 2005]

2006
Susan A. Ross
For the Beauty of the Earth

2007
M. Shawn Copeland
The Subversive Power of Love

2008
Barbara Fiand
Awe-Filled Wonder